CW00498098

The Martyr's Guide To Poison Tasting

By

Gary J. Fraboni

<u>Other Books By Gary J. Fraboni</u>

(insert cricket noise here)

The Martyr's Guide To Poison Tasting

By
Gary J. Fraboni

Two Leaf Clover Publishing

First Edition

ISBN: 978-0-578-13970-8

For

If you find someone who loves you
half as much as me,
you'll be twice as lucky as most.

Author's Note

This entire book was made
with 110 black pens and a razor blade.
Peace.

Welcome to
The Martyr's Guide to Poison Tasting
and other poems for the lonely.
Scratched and scribed and left to die
by Gary J. Fraboni.

Content of Tables

Canto IV

Side A (65)

Lollipop Street, A Music Box Filled With Dirt, March of a Million Lepers,
A Crabtacular Feast, Redolence, Kill Your Cell Phone, God of Atheists

Side B (74)

A Call To Arms, Red and Black Ghouls, Victor, Dance to the Dirge, Origami,
Counting Wolves, 2nd Coming of Noah, Black Goblin, Black Cats

Canto V

Side A (87)

Rainbow Chase, Haunted, Behind Those Locks, Un Remords de Ballon, Diamond Sea,
The Unkindness of Ravens, Greatest Science Project Ever, The Pit

Side B (98)

Others' Lives, Buddy, 200 Dollar Man, Little Tiny Footprints, In Dreams,
Jane and the Cerebral Garden, A Brush With Death

The Invited (Outro) (110)

The Appendix (112)

A Gallery of Broken Thoughts (115)

The Uninvited (Intro)

I'm throwing a party
with plenty of rum.
The uninvited are welcome to come.
I'm throwing a party
with balloons and cake.
The uninvited are welcome to take.
I'm throwing a party
with merrymakers and mimes.
The uninvited are coming this time.
I'm throwing a party
so don't push or shove,
for the uninvited to share in the love.

Canto I

"You be good, see you tomorrow. I love you"

- Alex (parrot) . 2007

Last words of Alex, an African grey parrot,
used for avian communication studies
at Harvard University for over 30 years.

Side A

Devil/Angel

Turn slowly sinner to saint.
Burn emotions when you paint.

Paint you when emotions burn.
Saint to sinner slowly turn.

Angel/Devil

Loss

I' ve been lost in this world
since the day I first lost you.
At a loss for words, lost in my thoughts
and lost on what to do.

True Love

My true love is rare

a thought in the air,

with hair the hue of a longing stare.

She whispers sweet

with the loveliest lips,

the same exact shade as strawberry sips.

She's tender and mild

with her feminine wile.

The color of cinnamon blended with style.

She's perfectly curved

for the optic nerve,

with a smile no man should ever deserve.

She's the first day of spring

when the nightingales sing.

The worthiest queen for the shiniest ring.

Her eyes are butterflies

deep in the forest,

The lullaby written in pigment is gorgeous.

It's meant to be.

She came from the sea.

If I was Poe, she's Annabel lee.

She makes me do flips

like sunken ships.

But my true love is unaware that I even exist.

The Necklace

I slaved on a necklace
for days and days.
It was entirely made
out of spiders' legs.
I searched high and low.
I searched close and vast.
I tied little knots
with a magnifying glass.
So many colors
for me to choose,
black widows, green lynx,
and a brown recluse.
I have to admit,
it wasn't all fun.
I once burned my thumb

in a golden sun.
Deep in a pit
where the glue spitters spit
and harvestman harvest
the heart of Charlotte,
I seized an unlucky shamrock
with tweezers and jars.
An orb in a jail
with toothpicks for bars.
Tangoed with tarantulas
entangled with floss.
Untangled the angles
of a St Andrew's cross.
Finally wrapped up,
my work all complete,
the perfect gift
for somebody sweet.
But when she opened the box
her screams unfurled,
I'm giving up trying
to understand girls.

8

The Fortune Teller Massacre

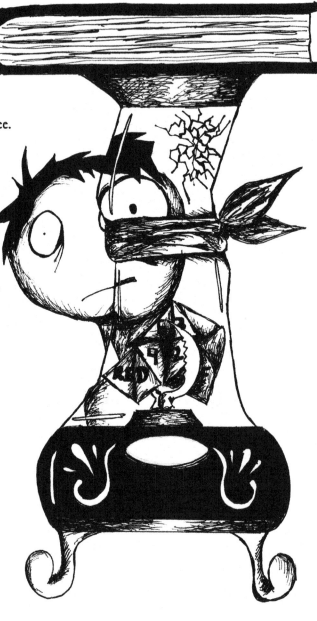

Sandy loves Johnny
and Sally loves Ronnie
and Michelle loves Brian McGee.
Jenny loves Dustin
but says that she doesn't.
But watches him by the tree.
Vickie asked Chris
for a hug and a kiss.
But secretly really loves Dee.
Michael loves Susie
and I love Julie
and Julie my dear loves

~~me.~~

9

The Last Apple Seed

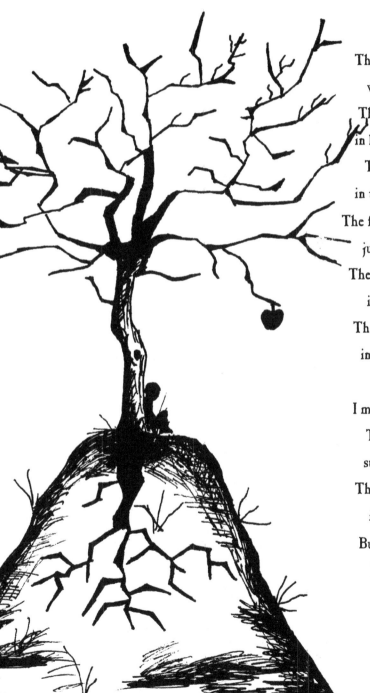

The first one I thought
was a black pebble.
The second one I split
in half with my shovel.
The third one I lost
in the muddiest puddle.
The fourth one was trouble,
just plain old rubble.
The fifth one disappeared
inside of the dryer.
The sixth one I dropped
in the thorniest briar.
The seventh one
I mistakenly swallowed.
The eighth one was
surprisingly hollow.
The ninth one I cooked
in a big tasty stew.
But the last apple seed
I planted for you.

Beautiful Halloween

He came from the sea on Halloween,

the only day when they wouldn't scream.

He met a girl the color of cream.

She thought it was cute his costume was green.

She was pristine with no seaweed to clean.

The night was the best or so it would seem.

Some teens took her bag because they were mean.

He split up his candy. They were a team.

They gave one another a shoulder to lean,

fell asleep in peace, lost in a dream.

The next morning was the most horrible scene.

When the sun arose, he froze and turned into steam.

11

Side B

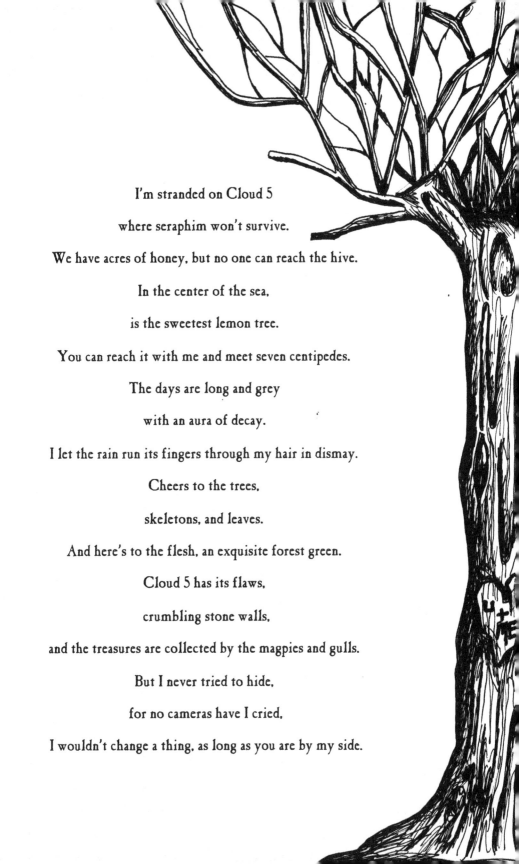

I'm stranded on Cloud 5

where seraphim won't survive.

We have acres of honey, but no one can reach the hive.

In the center of the sea,

is the sweetest lemon tree.

You can reach it with me and meet seven centipedes.

The days are long and grey

with an aura of decay.

I let the rain run its fingers through my hair in dismay.

Cheers to the trees,

skeletons, and leaves.

And here's to the flesh, an exquisite forest green.

Cloud 5 has its flaws,

crumbling stone walls,

and the treasures are collected by the magpies and gulls.

But I never tried to hide,

for no cameras have I cried,

I wouldn't change a thing, as long as you are by my side.

A Dragonfly's World

I live a dragonfly's world
attached to my girl.
We swirl through the air
in a stain glass whirl.
It's a wonderful show
I don't mean to gloat.
When I push she pulls,
but it keeps us afloat.
When sick and tired
and wings are on fire,
she flexes her might
and drives us higher.

And when she's exhausted
and needs to rest,
I flap even harder
and try my best.
Yes it's crazy
just me and my lady.
It's a lot of work
just to fly straightly.
I wouldn't trade it
to be a prince or a king
'cause when I can't fly
she is my wings.

How to Mend a Broken Heart

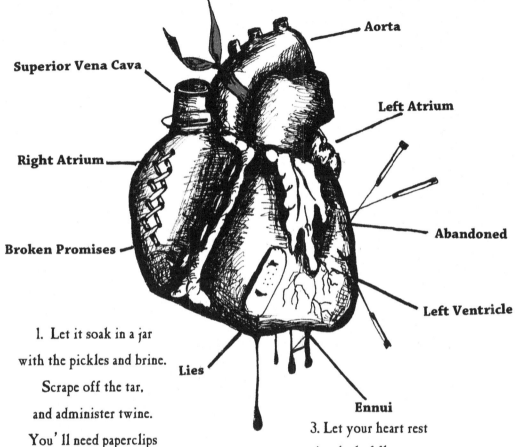

Aorta

Superior Vena Cava

Left Atrium

Right Atrium

Abandoned

Broken Promises

Left Ventricle

Lies

Ennui

1. Let it soak in a jar
with the pickles and brine.
Scrape off the tar,
and administer twine.
You'll need paperclips
to hold down the ventricles.
Maybe a glue stick
to control all the tentacles.

2. Now sew with a needle
of black widow's silk,
that's been coated in gold
in a thimble of milk.
Numb an atrium
with laudanum and some morphine
and inject it with Puerto Rican rum
and endorphins.

3. Let your heart rest
in a bed of flowers,
wet baby's breathe
for at least 12 hours.
Put it back in your chest
it should all be healed.
Restore the factory setting
by itself it should seal.

But don't sit and pout
if it's too much to do,
you could always go out
and find someone new.

16

X's and O's

X said to O, "Without us you should know

love surely cannot exist."

O said, "Without me it'd be L-V-E."

X said, "my point you have missed."

The Thing

There is a Thing that lives under your bed,
inside your closet, inside your head.
He nibbles your hair and tickles your feet.
He roughs up your bear and tugs at your sheet.
Unless you give him something to eat,
your worries and fears are his favorite treat.
The more you give, the more he takes,
until it's 4 a.m. and you're still awake.

18

Bad Taste

There is a rattlesnake,
he makes a mistake.
He falls for a maraca
'cause she knows how to shake.
Although she can move
and plays her part good,
her head is kind of hollow
and her heart pumps wood.

Canto II

"I take the poison bitter sips and smile big when I drink"

- Aesop Rock. "Bracket Basher". (2002)

Side A

A Lemming's Garden of Verses

I gave my crush some daisies.

She shoved them in my face.

She called me something crazy

and put me in my place.

I took the daisies back,

and tied them in a row.

I had the right knack,

to construct them in a bow.

I gave my crush a bow.

She shoved it in my face.

She screamed at me, "NO"

and put me in my place.

So I took the bow back

because I knew I'd only lose,

and I measured round my throat

and tied the daisies in a noose.

When The Sun Turns Black

I've been catching 50 fireflies
every single night.
Just in case the sun's
pilot light won't ignite.
I keep those slimy silkworms
stored inside my room.
When the penguins punch their clocks,
I'll have a warm cocoon.
I keep cicadas sequestered
in the basement by the hearth.
When melody meets the dodo,
I'll school them on Mozart.

I keep on counting roaches
in jars inside the attic.
When locusts eat their own,
I'll be dining here ecstatic.
I keep a nest of nymphs,
nestled in the chute.
For no good reason really,
I just think their kind of cute.
When the sun turns to black,
and it's finally the end.
I saved a seat for you
all I've wanted is a friend.

Garden of Broken Mirrors

Welcome to the Garden of Broken Mirrors
where every self-portrait is cracked.
It's confusing and unclear
when you aren't the one looking back.

Empty

Some little boys

threw away toys

and played with the empty box.

I threw away both

and played with the emptiness

left behind as thoughts.

1st Doll to Pull the Pins Out

You can call me names
and invade my brain.
Leave me out for the wolves
that hunt in the rain.
But you can't control me.
I am free.
You can twist in your pins
and get under my skin.
Throw me away in the bin
with the rubbish and tin.
But you can't control me.
I am free.

You can poke me and prod me
and try to Svengali.
Use a magnifying glass
to blacken my body.
But you can't control me.
I am free.
You can leave me to sour
like you have the power.
But I'm growing stronger now
with each passing hour
because the pins are out
and I'm finally me.

Valentine's Day

I'm staying in. I'm bolting the doors,
getting some work done, doing some chores,
cleaning the toilet, mopping the floors,
scrubbing my ears and cleansing my pores.
But I'm absolutely not going out on
Valentine's Day.
I'd rather stay home and puke and yack,
protest love all dressed in black,
sit on my couch and count the cracks
on my walls from front to back.
But I'm absolutely not going out on
Valentine's Day.

I'd rather sit home and watch the paint,
hold my breath till I start to faint,
or read up on my favorite saint.
But I ain't going out on
Valentine's Day.
I'd rather sit home and chew on pits
from cherries that have already been spit.
Oh, what did you say? You want to sit
at the park with me? Oh, I guess for a bit.

To Be or Not To Be ?

I know you won't understand this,
but I'd like to cut my own wrist.
But then I'd get blood on my brand new shirt,
and that would make me pissed.

29

Side B

30

The Reluctant Lord of Crows

At the onset of birth, they didn't know what they saw,

more straw than a boy,

more boy than a doll.

At school, children would spit and they'd tease.

They once fed his arm

to a dog and his fleas.

He went for a walk to reflect on his life,

but was kidnapped by farmers

with armor and knife.

They sewed his mouth shut and crucified him on sticks

in a meadow alone

with his thoughts and his wits.

Till the crows came and they sat by his side.

Adjusting his hat

and cleaning his eyes.

The crows were intrigued. They liked what they saw.

He provided them shade.

They played with his straw.

Till he passed away amongst the rows.

And was escorted to heaven.

Led by the crows.

The Martyr's Guide to Poison Tasting

So you wish to be a poison taster,
this you must know.
It's not all glamour, glitz,
excitement and show.
Arsenic is for the novice
if you don't mind cottonmouth.
With two shots or more
you get vodka on the house.
It has a slight hint of garlic

so no kissing here today.
If you don't follow my advice,
you'll be dead anyway.
Strychnine will make
your mouth salivate faster.
Introduce the bitterness
to Gouda and some crackers.
Anti-freeze is sweet.
Cobra venom is bitter.
So mix them in a blender
on the rocks before dinner.
I don't care for nightshade,
this I must say so.
With risotto they taste
like sun dried tomato.

Mantis

Death cap mushrooms
on pizza gourmet,
and curare goes well
with lemon sorbet.
Belladonna is sour
and works just fine
as a substitute for ginger
on chicken with wine.
Cyanide so sweet
with it's almond taste.
If you don't mind your heart,
at a hummingbird's pace.
Hemlock is delectable
in the spring of the year.
Just ask Socrates,
he enjoys it with beer.
I have recipes for saffron,
wolf's bane, and nickel,
poison frog legs,
and mercury sickles.
Take it from me
a poison taster for kings.
Never swallow the venom
and spit when you sing.

The Freaks

They come from their caves.

They come from their huts.

They come with their brats that sit on their guts.

They come to gawk.

They come to stare.

They come to the fair with their mangy hair.

They come for one reason. They come to enjoy.

The Freaks all come out to see Lobster Boy.

They rattle his cage.

They squint from the lights.

They're unruly and cruel and duel in some fights.

They point and they laugh.

They chortle and huff.

They drool from their chins with gristle and snuff.

They come for one reason. They come to enjoy.

The Freaks all come out to see Lobster Boy.

They say he's repugnant.

They spit and despise.

They see him distorted through crisscrossed eyes.

They throw at him dirt

and popcorn in pails.

They gesture crudely with cracked fingernails.

They come for one reason. They come to enjoy.

The Freaks all come out to see Lobster Boy

Canvas

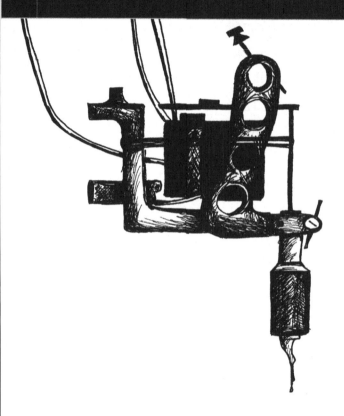

There was an illustrated man
with ink soaked in his skin,
with depictions of figments
on the pigments within.
His flesh was a gallery
where many tales were shown,
from the fairest of maidens
to the ugliest of crones.

Year after year
compositions had grown,
colors seeped through the surface
chewing marrow off the bone.
Every cell a canvas
no skin tone was shown,
'till he faded to the background
with no tale of his own.

Invisible Ink
(In One Breath)

I used to think

you're worth the ink

in every single syllable.

Now I think

you bring me to

the brink of being miserable.

In fact, I think

I'll sink my ink

for someone sweet and whimsical.

Or else I think

I'll drink my ink

and shrink until invisible.

Suicide Phoenix

She tries wire and rope,
fire and dope.
Everyday she rises
in a kaleidoscope.
She tries pistols and knives,
eating mistletoe pies.
Everyday in the fire
she stretches to rise.
She tries pills and bolts,
electric eel volts.
Everyday she rises
in a whirl of smoke.

She tries drowning in muck,
jumping out of a truck.
Everyday she rises
despite of her luck.
She tries razors to slash,
an alligator clash.
Everyday she rises
from the depths of the ash.
Why does she do it?
The trouble she gives.
Not for a wanting of death,
but longing to live.

Canto III

"I could stay awhile,
but sooner or later I'll break your smile"

-White Stripes "A Martyr for My Love for You". (2007)

Side A

An Existential Conversation

Snowflake One met Snowflake Two
and said, "Oh my god, I'm just like you!
How can this be? How can this be?
It's a scientific anomaly.
If we are special and unique like everyone else,
then are we unique? I must ask myself.

If all of us are unique and we are the same,
are we unique? Or are we just plain?
So is uniqueness plain if no one's the same?
Oh my god, it's hurting my brain!"
Snowflake Two had something to say,
"just hold me before we both melt away."

Closed till Revelations

on earth." ...il the number of their
I heard around t... ...eir brethren should
g creatures and ...e ...ven to be killed as t...
any angels, nu...ber ...e... ...he...
ds and thous...nd... ...2 ...en op...ed ...he sixth sea
with a lou... ...ke ...and ...old... ...e was a g...
b who was s...d to ...ti... ...he... ...ecame black
alth and wis...... ...m... ...ame like blo...
glory and ble...... ...f th... fell to the ea...
y creature i...... ...nter fruit w...
der the ea... ...y vanished li...
...in, saying, ...every moun...
...one and to ....from its pl...
...r and glory a...... ...rth and the g...
4 And the f...... ...the rich and
...n!" and the ... fo...... ...ve and free,
...the rocks of
the Lamb o...... ...e mountains
s, and I heard...... ...ide us from
...tures say, as wit...... ...ted on the thr...
...Come!" 2 And I saw, ...Lamb; 17 for
...horse, and its rider had ....This at last is bone of
...was given to him, and ...... and flesh of my flesh;
...ing and to conquer. ...she shall be called Woman,...
...he second seal, I ....erefore a man leaves his fath...
...creature say, ...her and cleaves to his wife, and th...
...other horse, ...re both naked, and were n...
...saying, "You may... ...erpent was more subtle...
...tted to tak... ...wild creature that th...
...en shou... ...and he called with a
...ven a g... ...angels who had been
...ird sea... ...the sea or the t...
...e say ...Come!" ...led the servants of our
...a black horse, a...... ...ed, a hundred and fo...
...ce in his h...n... 6 an... ...ou...every tri...
...to be ... ...oice in the ... ...welve thousand of
...iving ...ures s... ...udah, twe...e thou...
...for ...enarius... ...en, twelve th...sa...
...y ... a denarius;... ...welve thous...o of
...wine!" ...e thousand of the
...ne...the fourth sea... ...thousand of the

From the Revelation to Genesis

I want to write a song
that's as beautiful as you,
but it would take till Revelations
for me to see it through.
I would study every poem
from lachrymose to divine.
To inscribe the perfect tongue,
I'd live a thousand lives.
I'd write with many hands
till fingernails are dust.
A thousand shades of eye,
watching ghosts begin to rust.
Master every instrument
that's ever breathed with style.
To craft a melody so sweet,
it could tell me of your smile.
And on the dawn of judgment,
I hope the canticle is right.
I'd spend the day in Revelations
for paradise tonight.

44

The Most Beautiful Flowers

I never stop for Lilies.
Violets are mundane.
Roses are high maintenance.
Dahlias are a pain.
Irises are fickle.
Daisies drink the sun.
Petunias are all wilted.
What's a Chrysanthemum?
Ivies grow too wild.
Zinnias are too tall.
Wallflowers steal my heart.
They're the perfectest of all.

.

45

QUEENS
NYPD
42a
733735

20"

15"

10"

5"

0"

46

You' ll Never Be Pretty

Nothing to do

so you consume glue

till you' re skinny and blue and cannot chew.

But you' ll never be pretty like her.

You can bathe in bleach

lay out at the beach

for that perfect peach that' s just out of reach.

But you' ll never be pretty like her.

You can puff out your chest

stuff it into your dress

forever obsessed with looking the best.

But you' ll never be pretty like her.

Nothing to do

so I' ll give you a clue.

What' s really true is you' re pretty like you.

That' s why you' ll never be pretty like her.

48

Amor Eterno

If I was a vampire with fangs of barbed wire,
I would do something not very nice.
I'd kiss you and cuddle and nibble your jugula
biting without thinking twice.
It would taste like salt water but sweeter and hotter,
and warm the insides of my core,
with a slight touch of metal corroding on petals
of lantana fresh from the shore.
I'd cherish the seconds the saccharine nectar,
the rarest of desolate orchids.
With eyes closed tight in the shadows of night,
I'd love it no matter how morbid.
I know it is selfish the fact I would relish
an act so despicably true.
I'll risk the self loathing rather than knowing
a world that exist without you.
You're incredibly beautiful body is musical.
I wouldn't change a hair on your head.
Animation suspended till this earth is ended,
we'd walk together undead.
The pain it would bring such a terrible thing
for one to do to a friend.
But I'd have all of time to make you mine.
I promise you'll love me again.

49

Where the Valerian Grows

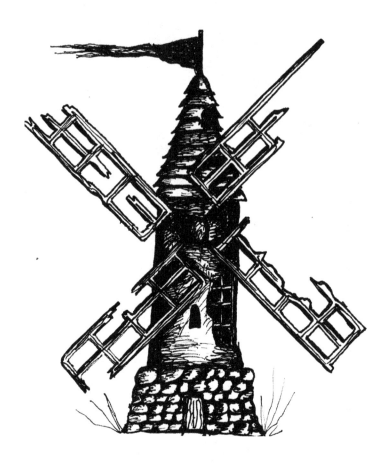

Wait for me by the windmill
where the wild valerian grows.
Where the whispers are warm and the water bugs swarm
in the quietest creek that flows.

Wait for me by the windmill
where the will-o-the wisp will grieve.
We'll hold one another till morning uncovers
and whisk away in the breeze.

The Best Way to Go

When I buy the farm,
I will do it with charm.
I won't fade to black in the sea.
Or expire by fire
electrocuted by wires
or succumb to a deadly disease.
No hit and run accident
or blood borne pathogen
will show this one to his maker.
No short circuiting brain
or a crash in a plane
will plan a date with the taker.
I won't be eaten by bears
or choke on a pear
or decay away in a coma.

I won't die of old age,
my body a cage,
submitting to the sarcoma.
No drugs nor bottle
nor botched sword swallow
will ever do me harm.
If you really must know,
the best way to go
is bleeding to death in your arms.

I Want To Know

I want to know what it's like to hold you,
only for an hour or so.
To feel your breath upon my chest,
I guess I'll never know.
I want to know the taste of your lips.
Are they bitter or sour or sweet?
Or is there a hint of vanilla and mint?
My wish is incomplete.
I want to know your voice
in the darkest hour of night.
Will it have a tone that seeps in my bones
and attempts to make everything right?

I want to know the touch of your skin
when no one else is around.
Can I make you quiver controlling shivers
connecting without a sound?
I want to know the beat of your heart
when it whispers in your chest.
Will it know my name and the reason I came?
Or speak to me in jest?
I want to know what it's like to be yours,
to see what we create.
To make two souls finally whole,
I guess I'll have to wait.

Side B

55

Behind the Black Curtain

I swear to you she dreamed

in 31 different flavors.

Till her inner thoughts

turned to tapeworms and razors.

She reinvented herself

to be well known and popular.

The truth didn't matter

if her mask was shown jocular.

She smiled for her friends,

but her heart was calamitous.

She borrowed personalities,

a social duck billed platypus.

She knew she was a fake,

slowly dying in the irony,

to the point where the poor thing

was lying in her diary.

Her old friends were gone.

Her new friends didn't care.

So she walks around with demons,

twirling fingers in her hair.

Sure she looks awake,

but for many many years,

she's been dreaming to herself,

and I'm the only one who cares.

POLICE LINE DO NOT CROSS   POLICE LINE DO   POLICE LINE D

Dear Butterfly

We loved you when you were a caterpillar.

You were sweet with a beautiful mind.

You were funny, charming, refined

certainly one of a kind.

Then you changed.

You became a butterfly full of pride.

You are still beautiful,

but I don't know what happened inside.

You allowed yourself

to be pinned behind glass,

for everyone to see.

Putting your wings on display

as gaudy as can be.

We worry about you.

I wish you remembered your worth.

We loved you when you were a caterpillar

your chrysalis glistened the earth.

When you are ready,

I'll help you take out the pins.

I'll clean your wounds with care

and wipe the blood from your skin.

You'll be free,

your wings will kiss the sky.

I promise my love, my dear, my sweet.

I would never lie.

The Pedestal

I placed you on a pedestal
trying not to be a pessimist.
The decision was regrettable.
It turned out to be a precipice.

58

Butcher Knife Ballet

You stab me in the back.
So I jab you in the heart.
You pirouette with butcher knives
to slice my life apart.
Our metal friend is in my gut
till I chassé into your chest.
I'm disgusted by the dark,
the mark I carve upon your breast.
You jerk the blade from bone
and fouetté right for my throat.
The vermillion spills so ill it fills
the pit up like a moat.
I'm exhausted from the coda.
Sweetheart, my blood is spent.
There's nothing left except for death,
the grandé reverence.
I'm withdrawing all my weaponry
and jeté away for peace.
This knife ballet we play all day
forevermore will cease.

59

Last Days of Lorelei

Even before you part your lips
and begin to utter hi,
my insides are being torn to bits
by vicious butterflies.
You can't fathom my absurdity.
I melt and wonder why.
I allowed myself to fall
for your winsome lullaby.
My nerves are pins and needles.
My heart's a thunder sky.
I tell myself I'm fine.
That's just another lie.
I sink into depression,
last days of Lorelei.

I want to strangle every specimen
in black formaldehyde.
I shiver from the thought
of the color of your eye.
To calm the beating wings,
I sip a cup of pesticide.
And if they are resilient
and persist to flutter by,
I'll swallow the whole bottle
till nothing is alive.

I'm Sorry For Everything
(even this poem)

— — — — — — — — — —

I said some things I didn't mean and meant some things I didn't say.

On another world, at another time,

I would ask about your day.

I could say I didn't mean to hurt you but that would be deceit.

I want your heart to beat

where pain and melancholy meet.

I couldn't untie the strings you interwove into my soul.

So I severed them instead

and emblazoned them in the coal.

You were the angel on my shoulder, and I shook you from my arm.

For the devil on my other,

knows only how to charm.

The safest place for you to be was in a desert by the sea.

Living out your dreams

a million miles away from me.

My one and only sin was how much I cared for you.

Now I'm sorting through aorta

with a tube of super glue.

I miss you so very much, probably more than anyone.

On the grayest days,

you were the color of my sun.

I meant some things I didn't say and said some things I didn't mean.

I hope we can be friends again

and not just in a dream.

61

J K L M O Q T U V W X Y Z B C F H

P.S. I wrote this open letter
with my bones sewn together.
If you wanna bend the seven sins again,
I'll wait for you forever.

62

Vinegar Hill

Hate is just love

that was left out to curdle.

On Vinegar Hill

marching backwards eternal.

Hate is just love

that was left out to wear.

On Vinegar Hill

in the stalest of air.

Hate is just love

that was left out to rust.

On Vinegar Hill

in the blackest of dust.

Hate is just love

that was left out to blight.

On Vinegar Hill

where you left me last night.

Canto IV

"Life is pain highness. Anyone who says differently
is selling something"

-The Man in Black, The Princess Bride. (1987)

Side A

Lollipop Street

A Music Box Filled With Dirt

On a small vacant planet exists a forgotten city.

By the city is a forest. Long ago was very pretty.

In the forest there's a path, a maze of a thousand thorns.

In the maze there is a hill, Mother Sun no longer warms.

On the hill there is a moat, with a dried up crystal stream.

On the stream there is a bridge, only crossed within a dream.

Near the bridge there is a castle, with crooked levels and floors,

and deep inside the castle there's a heavy metal door.

Through the door, there is a room that contains a wishing well.

At the bottom broken promises, from wishes that had fell.

And underneath the coins, a music box is smeared with dirt.

The music has been silenced as the gears no longer work.

If you took out every gear and replaced every pin,

you'll find my heart still plays a song. One you'll never hear again.

March of a Million Lepers

If you treat someone like dirt,
be weary of what might grow.
It might be the very wheat
that you have to sow.
And when the reaping is done
and you're still inflicting harm.
If you paint them all like lepers,
they might pick up their arms.
And when they're done rebuilding,
they'll march right to your town.
Don't be surprised my friend
when they burn you to the ground.

69

A Crabtacular Feast

The 1st annual fiddler crab convention
everyone gathers for this wondrous invention.
From all walks of life from south to east,
we sit and enjoy a crabtacular feast.
Squibble and squabble over who got the most
and stare with dead eyes at the last piece of toast.
It's the highlight of the show so nothing else matters.
They're giving the award for the biggest backstabber.

70

Redolence

She smells of cocoanut groves,
where gardenias grow
and new seasoned maple trees.
Where fresh water flows
and bread on a stove
heated in Parisian bakeries.
Of ripe orange peels
wisteria fields
rosewater and cinnamon sage.
Oceans of teal
and home cooked meals
and vanilla on rainy days.

Of begonia ravines
and orange jessamine
and Arabian jasmine vines.
Peppermint cream
geranium dreams
and lavender lavished in lime.
Of eucalyptus in aisles
4 o' clocks in a mile
and strawberries ached to be picked.
Chocolate soufflé to a child
it's so very vile
the smell of her makes me sick.

Kill Your Cell Phone

Before

After

Kill your cell phone. Let it die.
Put a bullet betwixt the eye.
Burn it in the brightest pyre
like a thousand Salem fires.
Kill your cell phone. Let it rot.
Let the circuits twist and clot.
Boil it in boric acid
till it bleeds the cheapest plastic

Kill your cell phone. Bring it silence.
Let it contract a dreadful virus.
Watch it fade to blackest sky
and laugh with joy if it begins to cry.
Kill your cell phone. Kill it dead.
Put a guillotine in its head.
Crush it till it becomes the wind.
Let your mind be free again

The God of Atheists

He creeps in while you sleep
and sits on your chest.
Looks you right in the eyes
and babbles in jest.
Says he's born of a wolf
and claws at your covers.
With blood on his brow
from slicing your mother.
He pulls out a needle
and rattles off quotes.
And shoves the long needle,
right down your throat.
You can't move a muscle.
Not even your wrists.
But the Atheist God,
does not exist.

73

Side B

A Call to Arms

Calling all losers, nerds, and rejects.
It's time for us to earn some respect.
Calling all geeks and dateless wonders.
It's time for us to shake with thunder.
Calling the last ones picked for the team
every bit worthy of hopes and dreams.
Calling the shy, the frail, and the weak,
wallflowers, the lonely, the pale and the meek.
Gather arms my friends for a cause that's just.
It's time for the world to pay attention to us!

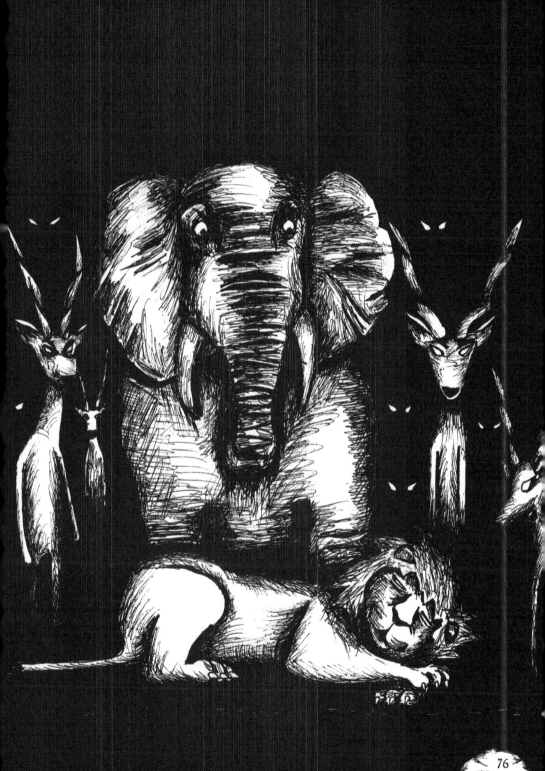

The strangest death occurred

in 1710

when a fool was condemned

to a ladybug den.

The insects when taken

by surprise

didn't flee in disguise. They devoured his eyes.

Millions and billions

of red and black ghouls

danced in the blood and splashed in the pools.

Nothing was left

but crimson and bones,

32 teeth and a kidney stone.

No one knows why they behaved that way.

No one believes what happened that day.

All I can say is one lady is fun,

but if another one comes,

I think that I'll run.

Red
&
Black
Ghouls

Victor

He had so many evil schemes
just to name a few.
He painted all the rainbows
a shade of black and blue.
He replaced the cartoons
with the daily news.
Melted freezie pops
and turned ice cream to glue.

Last Halloween,
he released a type of flu.
In the study with a pipe,
and we weren't playing "Clue".
Some people say he's crazy.
This also might be true.
He murdered 40 people
and cooked the bones in stew.

Dance to the Dirge

We slow dance in places
ghosts are afraid to tread.
We dance for those of ash
and those who are dead.
Raise your glasses high.
Poor wine for the unwanted.
We dance for yesteryear my dear.
We dance for the haunted.

We slow dance in places
wraiths are afraid to go.
Where memories are poached
by the vulture and the crow.
So pour yourself a toast.
The grapes are all but rotten.
We dance for yesteryear my dear.
We dance for the forgotten.

Origami

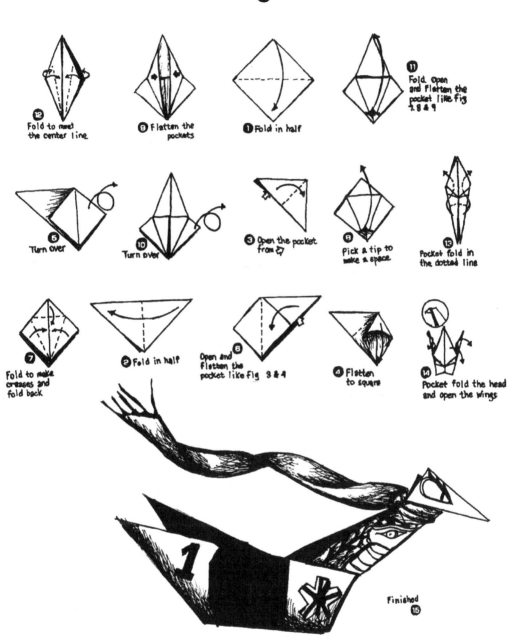

When I was little, I tried to make swans with origami.
I could never fold right.
They would take flight
as a swarm of kamikazes.

Counting Wolves

Last night
I just could not sleep.
So I closed my eyes
and counted sheep.
When I got to 93,
I thought I was done.
Then, I noticed something
peculiar with one.
She moved oddly
for a sheep,
and instead of a "baa"
she growled very deep.
So I inspected the others.
This can't be right.
Wolves in sheep clothing
the entire night!

2nd Coming of Noah

When god becomes an agoraphobe

and closes all the shades

and you can no longer spell warmth

with crayons of sunray.

I'll be the second coming of Noah

for this day and age.

Collect two of every cannibal

and let them out the cage.

I will charge admission.

It will be the greatest show.

Bring an extra pair of clothes

if you sit in the front row.

Black Goblin

I have a slight problem
you probably all know.
The blackest king of goblins
follows where I go.
He watches me all day.
He rummages my thoughts.
He's gazing at this page
wishing he was caught.
Now I have a thrill.
I'm no stranger to a battle.
This marks the day I kill
that doppelganger shadow.
All day I boxed the thing
till I slowed into a crawl.
I rocked the reddest rings
any saint had ever saw.
I devised the perfect plan
to end the demons life.
But I stopped myself and ran,
the goblin had a knife.
Then it occurred to me.
When I turn off all the lights,
he disappears you see
and is diverted from the fight.
I found a cave inside the park
where everything is black.
All day I sit amongst the dark
awaiting his attack.

Black Cats

Black cats were at my birth,
clawing the wet nurse there.
Black cats at my first kiss.
Her mouth was filled with hair.
Black cats when I left school
and went out on my own.
Black cats just sat and watched
when sewage filled my home.
Black cats when I felt love
made sure it didn't last.
Black cats sat back and laughed
when I walked on broken glass.
Black cats are still around.
I see them very often.
And when I kick the bucket,
the cats will lift the coffin.

Canto V

"I thought there' d be stars, We are abandoned"

- Marty (the stoner)
Cabin the the Woods. (2012)

86

Side A

Rainbow Chase

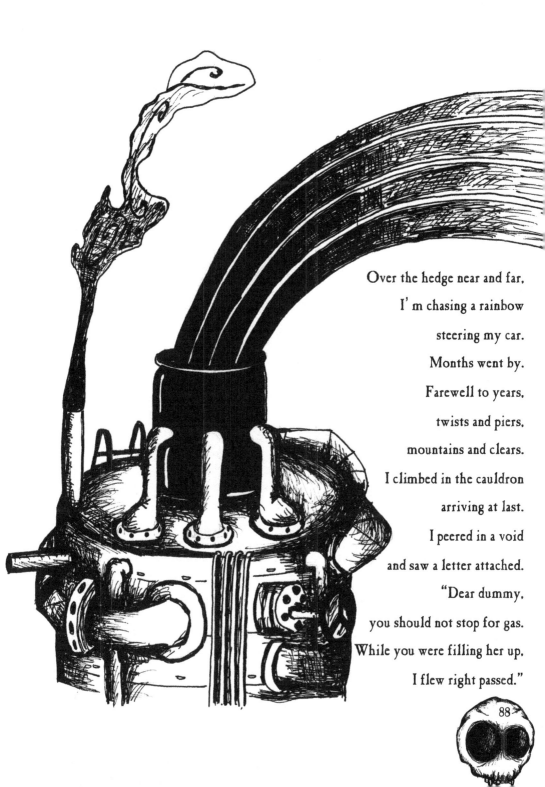

Over the hedge near and far,
I'm chasing a rainbow
steering my car.
Months went by.
Farewell to years,
twists and piers,
mountains and clears.
I climbed in the cauldron
arriving at last.
I peered in a void
and saw a letter attached.
"Dear dummy,
you should not stop for gas.
While you were filling her up,
I flew right passed."

88

Haunted

We traveled to the circus
when I was only five.
One clown melted sadness
with every step and stride.
He moved me to the point
I had goose bumps on my eyes.
I wished to meet the mummer
who kept the show alive.
They took me to his chambers
moving quickly on my toes.

Passing faces twisted
as tumors on a rose.
Not aware of any danger,
arabesque door ajar.
I peaked upon a stranger
grotesque and so bizarre.
What I saw that night still haunts me.
I lay awake in grief.
When the clown wiped off his makeup,
no face was underneath.

Behind Those Locks

There was an old man
who sits behind locks.
He sits all day
and talks to rocks.
"Black folks steal
and brown folks smell.
White and yellow folks
are all going to hell.

Red folks hate
and all folks kiss.
And purple people
don't even exist."
So one day he died,
right behind those locks,
and no one cried
not even the rocks.

Un Remords De Ballon
(From Brooklyn to France)

I escaped your grasp,
The unending clasp.
Riding a draft
through a cactus patch.
Right through the thorns
of the awfullest trees.
I waltzed with the bees
in a tumultuous breeze.
I flew with umbrellas
through rockets and pellets.
I flew with love letters
through chopper propellers.

I saw a new world
through my erratic dance.
Taken by chance
from Brooklyn to France.
Now what can I do
but stare in the blue?
Regretting my choice
and longing for you.

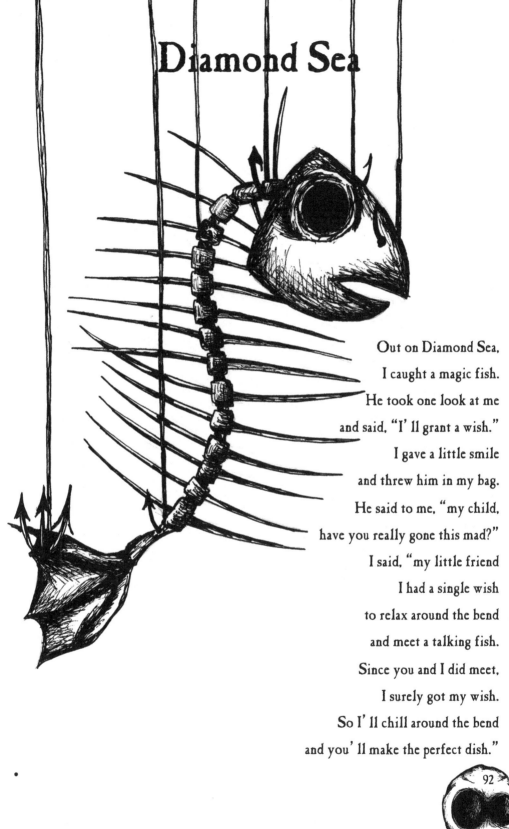

Diamond Sea

Out on Diamond Sea,
I caught a magic fish.
He took one look at me
and said, "I'll grant a wish."
I gave a little smile
and threw him in my bag.
He said to me, "my child,
have you really gone this mad?"
I said, "my little friend
I had a single wish
to relax around the bend
and meet a talking fish.
Since you and I did meet,
I surely got my wish.
So I'll chill around the bend
and you'll make the perfect dish."

92

The Unkindness of Ravens

An old man once said to me...

"If you ever see a cobra quiver,

It's just not your day.

If you ever see a shark shiver,

swim the other way.

But nothing compares to the unkindness of ravens.

Parrots make good company.

Sparrows make good hosts.

Finches have their charm.

Watch nightingales close.

But nothing compares to the unkindness of ravens.

The shrewdness of apes

is legendary in some books.

There is no adversary

for a parliament of rooks.

But nothing compares to the unkindness of ravens.

Wild cats cause destruction.

Rhinos are a crash.

Tigers will ambush you.

Avoid a plague of rats.

But nothing compares to the unkindness of ravens.

Foxes often skulk

in the glow of the moon.

Never rhumba with a rattlesnake

or gaze at a raccoon.

But nothing compares to the unkindness of ravens."

Then I asked the old man why,

and this is what he said,

"To suffer the unkindness of ravens

means that you are dead."

Greatest Science Project Ever

Oh dear, oh my, it's science fair time
and just my luck
I'm in my prime.
I think I'll kick back and take my time
and build my very own Frankenstein.
When it came to cadavers,
nothing did matter.
With a gall bladder from an African adder.
Epiglottis from an ostrich,
I know it's preposterous.
Esophagus from an endangered rhinoceros.
Scoured the canopies
in search of some manatees.
Proximal phalanges right from the Ganges.

The next part was smelly.
I caught a live skunk
for his bronchomediastinal trunk.
Subdeltoid bursa from Persia
and also right by this
maxillary sinus from ibis in Cyprus.
I have to be honest that no one can top this.
The xiphoid process
from conquests in Loch Ness.
I unearthed a tapir donated by neighbors
with a near perfect zygomaticus major.
Found a fornix in bricks from a Pekinese mix
and a useless appendix from popsicle sticks.
From a Great Dane, found a fibular frame
and also a retromandibular vein.
The finishing touch on my Frankenstein
an obiculous orb from porcupine.
After all my work, this I must say so,
I lost to a vinegar soda volcano.

The Pit

I watched sheep try to jump a pit

by and by.

They would leap for the sky,

plummet and then die.

Eventually, the pile of fleece

grew so high.

I could tiptoe on wool

to reach the other side.

97

Side B

Others' Lives

Have you ever wondered
about other's lives?
What sits in their head
controlling their eyes?
What makes them laugh?
What makes them cry?
What creeps down their spine
to explore insides?

There is a girl
near Sunny Side Drive,
selling blackbird pies
they're 2 for 5.
What goes on
inside of her mind
when those hypnotize eyes
begin to rewind?

Buddy

No one wants
to play with Buddy.
He smells like pee
and silly putty.
A beer bottle cap
is lodged in his eye.
It's rusty and sharp
and makes little girls cry.
Someone deranged
scribbled profanity
on his back with a sharpie.
Oh the humanity!
His right arm was eaten
by ravenous black birds.
Pull on the string

he sings Latin backwards.
His batteries leak
and melt through your pants
and half of his head
is infested with ants.
His model recalled
back in 79.
The design when reclined
would drip turpentine.
But, Buddy is cheerful,
though his life is quite meager.
And to be honest,
he don't wanna
play with you either.

FREE OR Best
OFFER
(So basically free)

200 Dollar Man

It happened so fast
all in a flash,
a thunderous smash
followed by crash.
A car tried to pass.
He slammed on the gas.
The aftermath was metal and glass.
Surgeons attached
his jaw with a latch
and fitted his cap
with an aluminum hatch.
They hacked and they beavered
with scalpels and cleavers.
His nervous receivers
were green pipe cleaners.
One microscope eye,
an alpine thigh,
a street pole sign

inclined in his spine.
His cochlea drum
was replaced by gum.
The "Tonka" folks sprung
for some of his lung.
The ligaments that broke
were bicycle spokes
with little bits of rope
to tighten his throat.
His veins were maintained
with miles of chains.
His heart, a toy train,
left out in the rain.
Physicians explained
life won't be the same.
With plain silly putty,
imprinting his brain.
With no insurance to own,
it's all they could condone,
and the doctor went home
spending more on his phone.

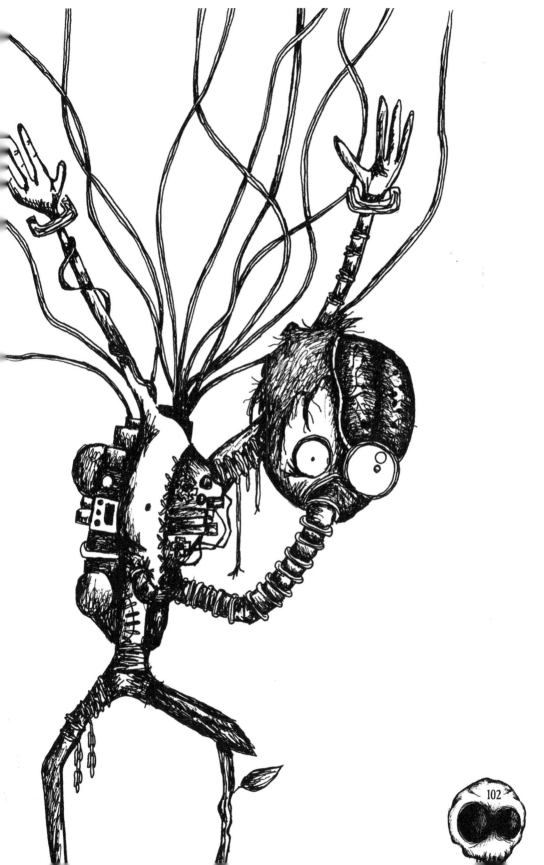

102

Little Tiny Footprints

Little tiny footprints,
I followed down the stairs.
Little tiny footprints,
I followed them in pairs.
I followed over here.
I followed over there.
They were on the toilet seat
peaking in the mirror.
I followed through the attic
over gowns and antiques.
Followed over barbells
that help with your physique.
They jumped on old toys
covered now with dust.
Over love letters
that often speak of trust.
They scamper to a box
where something there is hidden.
And run away scared
they know that it's forbidden.
Then down the darkest hall,
you'll never guess what I saw?
Those little tiny footprints,
led right up the wall.

103

In Dreams

An upstanding citizen
who never breaks the law.
Pacifist indeed,
from grace he never falls.
But every third moon,
he sleep walks the halls
dragging behind him
a set of bloody claws.
He has no memory
not one bit at all.
But wonders why red stains
decorate his lovely wall.

Jane and The Cerebral Garden

One morning, when Jane

awoke from her bed,

a garden of wonder arose from her head.

Forever the optimist,

she arrived on the scene,

a curious oddity, a botanist's dream.

Dragon fruit gleamed

with actual flame

and reversible tulips to keep out the rain.

It contained Venus flytraps

that snarled and barked

and star fruit that shined when lost in the dark.

I remarked on the oranges

that crept and crawled

and one I recall looked like a beach ball.

And best of all

you wouldn't believe,

a small team of fairies tended the leaves.

It seemed the garden

was splendid for Jane.

Till Johnny tugged on it and out popped her brain.

A Brush with Death

Little Susie was found by Old Miller Pond.
Her golden hair no longer blond.
Her fingernails black
and her teeth were green.
When asked where she was,
she said, "in a dream,
I was tied to a chain with a great black ball.
A small fish came, his nose was a saw.
He cut me free from my imprisoning moat.
When I came to the surface,
I was hit by a boat.

I drifted to black and misplaced my breath.

When I opened my eyes, I was looking at Death.

He said, 'my dear, I'll be be punished for this.'

And brushed back my hair and gave me a kiss.

Right on the cheek, of the watery floor,

lifted me gently and took me to shore.

He pulled out my soul from an emerald jar.

Whispered into my lungs and ignited a star.

I coughed up the seaweed, the water, the crud,

the filth and the grime, the pain and the blood.

Death went to the water lost in a wave.

Now, I think I'm ok, so how was your day?"

Now I think I'm ok, so how was your day?
Now I think I'm ok, so how was your day?
Now I think I'm ok, so how was your day?
Now I think I'm ok, so how was your day?
Now I think I'm ok, so how was your day?
Now I think I'm ok, so how was your day?
Now I think I'm ok, so how was your day?
Now I think I'm ok, so how was your day?
Now I think I'm ok, so how was your day?
Now I think I'm ok, so how was your day?
Now I think I'm ok, so how was your day?
Now I think I'm ok, so how was your day?
Now I think I'm ok, so how was your day?
Now I think I'm ok, so how was your day?
Now I think I'm ok, so how was your day?
Now I think I'm ok, so how was your day?
Now I think I'm ok, so how was your day?
Now I think I'm ok, so how was your day?
Now I think I'm ok, so how was your day?
Now I think I'm ok, so how was your day?
Now I think I'm ok, so how was your day?

111

The Invited (Outro)

Charlatans and harlots and harlequin starlets
we'll forgive you if you fell.
If there's a story to tell and smoke to exhale,
we'll throw our coin to your well.
Looters and shooters and Buddha consumers
can come and lime on the stoop.
If your mind is divine and you know how to shine,
you're welcome to the group.
No gutter or mother or color or other
will we discriminate.
If you have a good heart and wood that will spark,
we'll set fire to the gate.

About the Author

Gary J. Fraboni is the last piece of hay
in a stack full of needles
writing backwards in the steeples
of medieval cathedrals.

113

Appendix

"Devil/Angel"- The entire poem is a palindrome. It's the same poem both forward and backward. "Turn slowly sinner to saint. Burn emotions when you paint. Paint you when emotions burn. Saint to sinner slowly turn." Read it backwards if you don't believe me.

"Loss"- The illustration is of a pickled punk. This is a mutated creature that was placed in a jar to appear in a freak show. In this case, it's a two-headed bear. One of the heads has recently died, leaving the other head eternally alone in the jar.

"The Necklace"- All of the spiders mentioned in the poem are real species of spiders. Except for Charlotte of course, which is a reference to EB White's Charlotte's Web.

"True Love"- "Annabel Lee" is a poem by Edgar Allen Poe in which his childhood love dies in a kingdom by the sea. They were murdered by angels because they were jealous of Poe and Annabel's love, and bored apparently.

"1st Doll to Pull the Pin Out"- Svengali is a character from the George Du Maurier novel Trilby. The character has become synonymous with someone who manipulates others for personal gain.

"Stranded on Cloud 5"- The title is a reference to the phrase "cloud 9" which is an idiom for perfect happiness. Cloud 5 lies somewhere between ennui and melancholia on the mood spectrum.

"A Dragonfly's World"- When dragonflies mate, they will fly around attached to one another.

"X's and O's" The X's and O's refer to hugs and kisses. If you didn't get that, you are just like "O".

"A Lemming's Garden of Verses"- A lemming is a small rodent famous for committing suicide. Scientists, however, have proven that this is only a myth. The title refers to the Robert Louis Stevenson poetry collection, A Child's Garden of Verses, which is similar to this poetry collection but with less porcupines and surprisingly little blood.

"The Martyr's Guide to Poison Tasting"- The illustration is of a mantis. After a mantis mates with a female, the female will bite off the head of the male and devour the corpse. This makes a male mantis a distinct martyr in the animal kingdom. The poisons mentioned in the poem are accurately described with taste and initial effect on the human body.

"Suicide Phoenix"- A phoenix is a mythological bird. When it dies, it is reborn again from fire. It can be in a constant cycle of death and rebirth. It's fun for the whole family.

"To Be or Not to Be?"- The title refers to Hamlet's famous soliloquy in which he contemplates suicide. At least I think that's what it's about. Who knows with all the word play and double entendres in Shakespeare plays?

"From the Revelation to Genesis"- "The Revelation" mentioned in the poem is a reference to the biblical revelation and last book of the New Testament, which would mark the end of time and the coming apocalypse. Genesis refers to the first book of the Old Testament and the Garden of Eden. Sometimes, you have to go through hell to reach paradise.

"Where the Valerian Grows"- Valerian is a flowering plant. Its roots are used to promote sleepiness. It's one of the key ingredients in Valium.

"Butcher Knife Ballet"- Many of the terms used are real ballet terms. The grande reverence is the final bow when the dance is complete.

"I'm Sorry For Everything"- The hangman puzzle is a real puzzle. It can be solved using the letters that are not there.

"A Crabtacular Feast"- Fiddler crabs are known to pull each other down when they are in a bucket to keep each other from escaping. Fiddler crabs are jerks.

"Fragrance"- 4' o clocks are a type of sweet smelling flower.

"Dance to the Dirge"- A dirge is a slow somber song played or performed at a funeral to express lament.

"The Unkindness of Ravens"- A group of ravens is called an unkindness. All of the animals mentioned have their scientific group name hidden within the poem. For example, a group of sharks is called a shiver.

"Greatest Science Project Ever"- All of the terms used are real anatomy terms. This doesn't necessarily mean that each animal has that particular part of the body though. I've never asked a skunk if he has a bronchomediastinal trunk.

"Diamond Sea"- The poem is a play on the Russian folk tale "The Fisherman and the Fish" in which a fisherman catches a golden fish that grants him three wishes and everyone goes home happy- probably.

"200 Dollar Man"- The poem is a parody of the 70's TV show "The Six Million Dollar Man", in which the character Steve Austin is injured in an experimental spaceship crash and rebuilt using state of the art technology. The 200-dollar man is rebuilt with junk that's lying around.

"Little Tiny Footprints"- Spoiler alert. They're ghosts.

116

A Gallery of Broken Thoughts

deleted poems, abandoned ideas, sketches
and other nonsense
not good enough for the main section

Creature

The creature asked a girl out at the mall.

She said, "no way in hell, no way at all."

He thought to himself, "she doesn't like me I'm small."

So he got himself a hammer

and bought himself a saw.

He built the perfect stilts, a way to make himself tall

and practiced all day so he wouldn't fall.

The next day he tried double or nothing with cupid.

She said, "It's not because you're short,

it's because you're creepy and stupid."

Roy Vs. Lynn

ROY ∞ LYNN

VS

Sometimes I feel sorry for Roy.
He thinks he's a real boy.
He's doesn't know
he is a malfunctioning toy.

Sometimes I feel for sorry for Lynn.
She's a doll of porcelain
with a computerized rim
and rubber for skin.

The Miraculous Mr. Cobwebs, eccentric to say the least.
In an electric chair he dines on his hair
and combs through spaghetti with feet.
The Amazing Mr. Cobwebs, has a collection of little black marbles.
Old pieces of gum and wampum drums
and chews on sticks of charcoal.
The Enchanting Mr. Cobwebs, the reason the Titanic sunk.
When his head spins, he's charming his friends,
an army of zombified skunks.
The Exquisite Mr. Cobwebs, all the children stay away.
He bleeds oil spills to kill baby seals
and asks shadows on the ceiling to play.
The Remarkable Mr. Cobwebs, he crawled right out of the sea.
His veins filled with mud, balloons filled with blood.
Beware of this man for he's me!

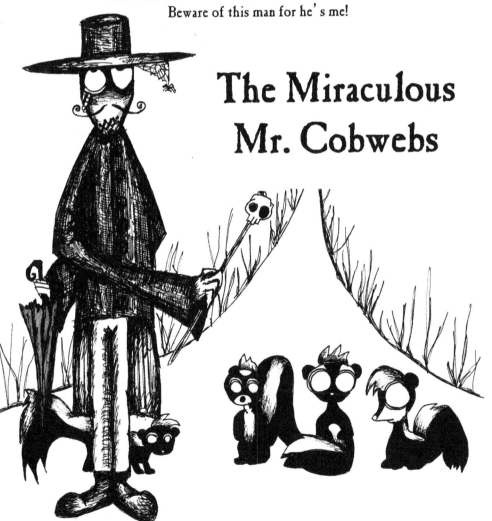

The Miraculous
Mr. Cobwebs

Treasure

Help the poet find the TREASURE

EXIT

I found a treasure map
But it's all torn apart
If I'm not mistaken
It's a map to _____'s heart
The problem is it's all in bits
With barbed wire paths and cottonmouth pits
A never ending dead end of crypts
A shattered in fifth labyrinth
I'm not sure if it's worth the risk
If a clear path even exists
One thing for sure I understand
If I could piece it together
With a wonderful plan
If I could glue the shards best I can
If I could get _____'s treasure in hand
I could open the chest and be nothing less
Than the richest one in the land

Snake Oil

Come one come all
snake oil for sale!
Just this hour
two dollars a pail
What did you say?
What does it do?
What doesn't it do, I'll give you clue
Give me your duckets,
2 for seven
And this elixir mixed
will get you to heaven
I have a serum that kills all the fleas
For 50 cents more it cures all disease
Right now if you buy the warranty
You'll make back your money guaranteed
And this little bottle,
throw away your speedo
This antidote will boost your libido
Oh and this a truth serum
cheapest and fair
See (gulp)
Actually you'll be lucky
if you don't lose your hair

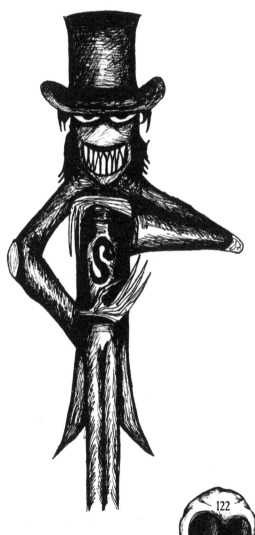

122

Stranded on Cloud 5 Alternate

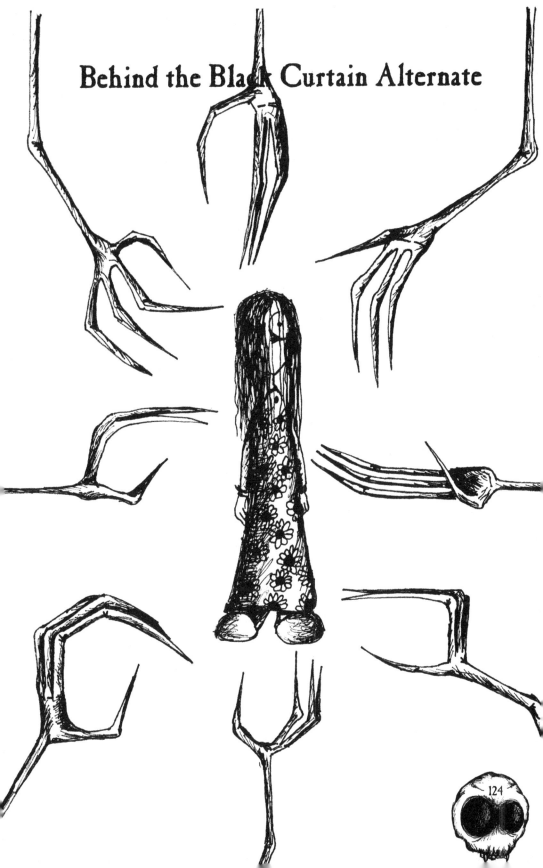

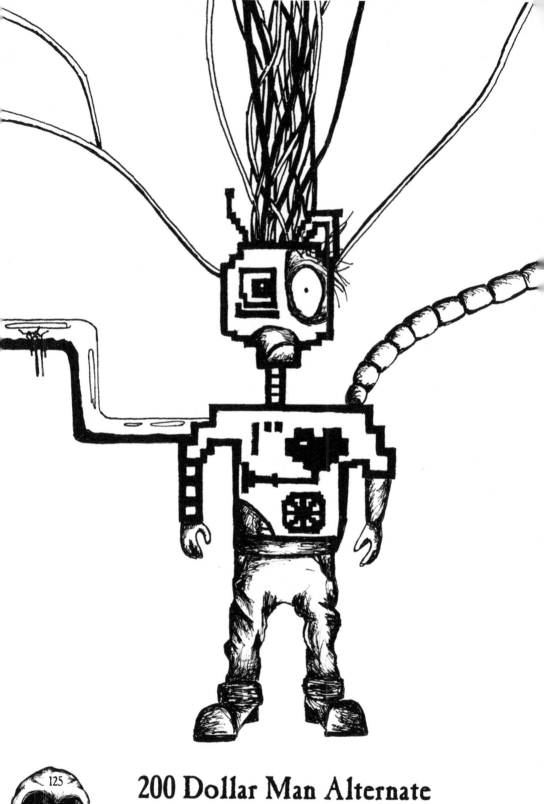

200 Dollar Man Alternate

True Love Alternate

True love

notme (someguy)

127

The Necklace Alternate

LOLLIPOPS to.

Scavengirlla

129

The Smudge

Nothing to
do

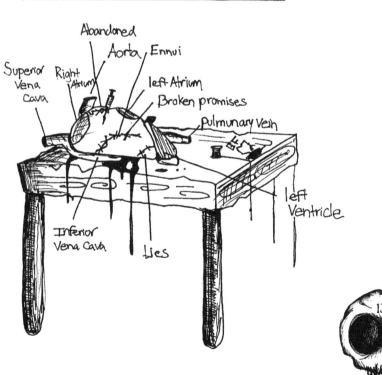

Abandoned

Aorta · Ennui

Superior Vena Cava · Right Atrium · left Atrium

Broken promises

Pulmonary Vein

left Ventricle

Inferior Vena Cava · Lies

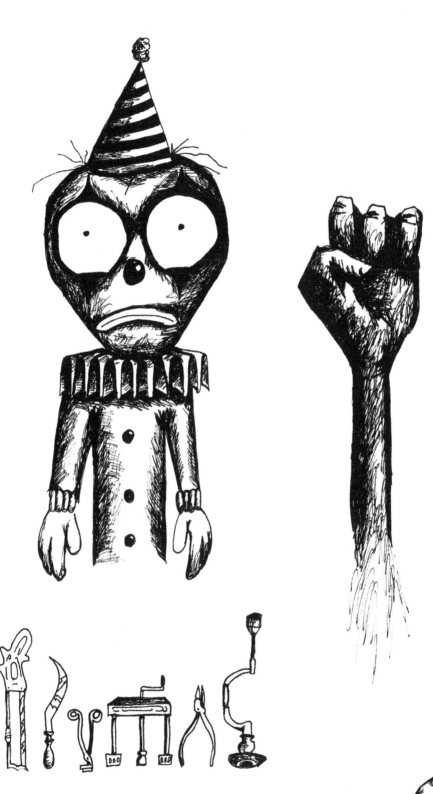

135

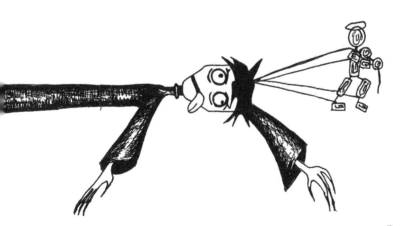

3

1

2

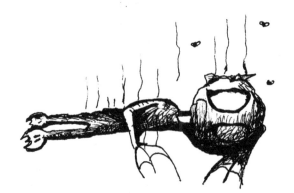

137

4

The Martyr's Guide to Poison Tasting

And Other Poems For the Lonely

By Gary J Fraboni

Scratched and Scribed and left out to die

Bye

Lightning Source UK Ltd.
Milton Keynes UK
UKOW01n1406050318
318906UK00001B/129/P